Plant-Based
COMFORT FOOD
CLASSICS

· ·

SIMPLE AND NOURISHING VEGAN DISHES

SANDRA

Skyhorse Publishing

Library of Congress Cataloging-in-Publication Data is available on file.

Cover design by Daniel Brount
Cover photographs by Sandra Vungi

Print ISBN: 978-1-5107-6496-5
Ebook ISBN: 978-1-5107-6869-7

Printed in China

CONTENTS

INTRODUCTION

I have been passionate about cooking since I was five years old. I used to watch my mom prepare delicious meals for our family of five, and something about the art of food making fascinated me so much that I decided to roll up my sleeves and heat up the pots and pans.

I haven't stopped since. My love for creating recipes and great home-cooked meals, and seeing people's happy faces when they eat my food, is bigger than ever. I have dreamed about my very own cookbook since my early youth. When I became a vegan in 2007, it was clear to me that my passion for food and compassion for animals were meant to work together. I started my own vegan recipe site in 2009. In 2012, my first cookbook with one hundred vegan recipes was published by a major publisher in my home country of Estonia. In 2013, I created vegansandra.com to share my recipes in English.

I also run my own little catering company, which has allowed me to create so many delicious recipes, suitable for both fabulous parties and for fun, casual times with family and friends. This cookbook contains only the best selection of amazingly tasty food that will make your family and friends fall in love with these new, yet still comforting, tastes. Believe me, they will talk about your party for a long time—whether they're vegan or not!

This comprehensive vegan cookbook provides an array of dinner party fare, from soups, salads, and spreads to main dishes and cakes. You can even find a whole selection of dreamy no-bake desserts as well as barbecue and Christmas specials. The recipes in this book are doable and affordable and are made with familiar ingredients that you can find in your local grocery store—no fancy, complicated, and expensive ingredient lists. The dishes are home-style, flavorful, and quite filling. All these recipes are also perfectly suitable for a cozy family dinner if you are not in the mood to throw a party. Since I am an Estonian, there are also quite a few special Estonian recipes like curd pastry with raisins, Estonian cookie cake, black pudding sausages, and sauerkraut with barley.

I hope you will find some inspiration and feel the same amount of happiness when cooking delicious, compassionate, and healthy food for the people you care about. I wish you the greatest tasty moments and loveliest memories!

—Sandra Vungi

TIPS FOR VEGAN COOKING

- When I mention the word "vegan" in some ingredients (like "vegan margarine," "vegan puff pastry," or "vegan chocolate"), it simply means that it doesn't contain any animal ingredients. Sometimes, supposedly vegan products can contain animal ingredients. Carefully read the labels.

- I like to use light soy sauce in my recipes, not the thick and dark sauces. You can also use low sodium or tamari soy sauce if possible.

- Quite a few of my recipes ask for a vegetable stock powder. I use one with only salt, dried vegetables, and herbs in it. No additional stuff. Some store-bought vegetable stocks can contain flavor enhancers and other unnecessary ingredients. Try to avoid those. You can also replace the stock powder with a little bit of salt.

- If you are low on money, soaked and blended sunflower seeds are a great alternative to cashews to make creamy sauces, soups, and spreads.

- Some of my recipes ask for "vegan cream." It is basically an alternative to regular light cream to make some dishes and sauces creamier. I like to use soy-based cream, but you can definitely try different ones. And if you are not a fan of store-bought creams, just use some homemade cashew or sunflower seed cream. It will work in most of the recipes.

- The only special cooking utensil you need in some of these recipes is a hand blender. All my creamy soups, spreads, and sauces are blended with this affordable and effective gadget.

SOUPS,
SALADS,
SNACKS,
AND
SPREADS

CHEESY PUMPKIN AND CAULIFLOWER SOUP

For me, this soup is such eye-candy. And the belly will be happy too! It has a smooth texture, a beautifully vibrant color, and a slightly cheesy taste. It's like sunshine on your party table!

Serves 3–4

- 1¾ pounds pumpkin flesh (peeled and seeds removed)
- ½ head of cauliflower
- 4 Tablespoons oil
- 1 teaspoon salt
- ground black pepper to taste
- 1½ cups hot water
- 3–4 Tablespoons nutritional yeast
- ½ teaspoon turmeric
- ¾ teaspoon vegetable stock powder
- 1 Tablespoon soy sauce

Preheat the oven to 400°F. Grease a medium-sized baking pan. Add pumpkin cubes, cauliflower florets, oil, salt, and pepper. Bake until the pumpkin is soft. Place the baked pumpkin and cauliflower into a pot; add hot water, nutritional yeast, turmeric, vegetable stock powder, and soy sauce. Stir, bring to a boil, and remove the heat. Blend until smooth.

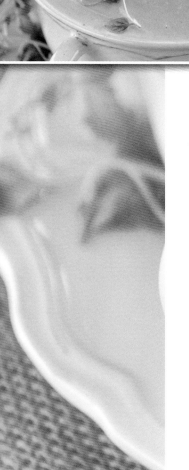

CREAMY ONION AND PLUM SOUP

There is this great children's book I love to read once in a while. A tiny fella named Viplala is the main character and he gets into all sorts of trouble. But since I have always been a foodie, I especially like the fact that a character in this book worked in a factory where they produced savory canned plum soups! How amazing is that? I just had to create my own plum soup recipe, and it came out so tasty. Long live the children's books with their creative ideas!

Serves 4–6

- 2 Tablespoons oil
- 2 Tablespoons vegan margarine
- 8 medium onions
- pinch of salt
- pinch of ground black pepper
- 24 ounces plum compote (keep the liquids)
- 4¼ cups hot water
- 1 teaspoon dried thyme
- 1 Tablespoon balsamic vinegar
- ½ Tablespoon vegetable stock powder
- 4 Tablespoons soy sauce
- ½ cup vegan cream
- fresh parsley for garnish

Heat oil and margarine in a thick-bottomed pot. Add sliced onions, salt, and pepper. Cook for about 5 minutes. Pit the plums if needed and add them to the onions. Also add the plum compote liquids and hot water. Boil for a couple of minutes and add thyme, balsamic vinegar, vegetable stock powder, and soy sauce. Boil until the onions are soft. Add vegan cream and boil for another couple of minutes. Add fresh parsley, bring to a boil, and remove the heat. Serve the soup with crispy toasted buns.

RICH BEAN AND TOMATO SOUP WITH PASTA

*My sister Hedvig and I both love red food. We love to dream about beet salad or pasta sauce or this rich bean and tomato soup. Actually, this soup is perfect **after** the party, if you know what I mean.*

Serves 4–6

- 3 Tablespoons oil
- 3 onions
- ¾ teaspoon salt
- 4 cloves of garlic
- 2 bay leaves
- 2 potatoes
- 4 cups water
- 1 cup uncooked pasta (seashell for example)
- 3 teaspoons vegetable stock powder
- 2 teaspoons brown sugar
- 2 teaspoons paprika powder
- pinch of ground black pepper
- 2 (14-ounce) cans tomatoes
- 1 (14-ounce) can white beans, drained and rinsed
- ¾ Tablespoon apple cider vinegar
- 2 Tablespoons soy sauce
- fresh herbs for garnish

Heat oil in a thick-bottomed pot and add chopped onions and salt. Cook for 3 minutes. Add chopped garlic and bay leaves. Cook for about 30 seconds. Now add the potato cubes and water. Boil for 3 to 4 minutes. Add pasta, vegetable stock powder, brown sugar, paprika powder, and ground black pepper. Boil until the pasta is almost soft. Add canned tomatoes, canned white beans, apple cider vinegar, and soy sauce. Boil for 2 to 3 minutes. Garnish with finely chopped fresh herbs.

CURRIED CHICKPEA AND AVOCADO SALAD

This is my dream salad. It has been a huge hit at my cooking workshops and private parties. It's creamy, juicy, crunchy, and filling!

Serves 6–8

- 2–3 Tablespoons oil
- 2 (14-ounce) cans canned chickpeas, drained and rinsed
- 2 Tablespoons curry powder
- 3 Tablespoons soy sauce
- 2–3 ripe avocados
- 1 ripe pomegranate
- head of iceberg lettuce (about 1½ pounds)
- couple of handfuls cherry tomatoes, halved
- 1½ cups vegan mayo
- couple of handfuls fresh basil

Heat oil in a pan. Add chickpeas and cook for 2 to 3 minutes. Add curry powder and soy sauce. Mix and cook for a couple minutes. Remove from heat.

Pit the avocado and slice it. Slice the pomegranate in half and carefully squeeze and scrape out the seeds. Chop the lettuce. Mix the avocado, pomegranate seeds (leave some for garnish), lettuce, cherry tomatoes, and fried chickpeas with vegan mayonnaise. Add some soy sauce if needed. Garnish with fresh basil leaves and pomegranate seeds. Serve immediately.

FRESH SALAD WITH SALED PEANUTS

This salad is my favorite in the summer. It's so light and fresh yet also quite filling with the salted peanuts included. Feel free to add any fresh veggies of your choice to make it even more colorful.

Serves 8–10

Salad:
- 2 ripe tomatoes
- 1 medium cucumber
- 1 (5-inch) piece of leek
- medium head of Chinese cabbage
- a few handfuls of arugula
- 1 cup salted peanuts

Dressing:
- 2 Tablespoons quality oil
- ½ teaspoon salt
- pinch of ground black pepper
- 2 Tablespoons water
- 3 Tablespoons pineapple or orange juice

In a large bowl, mix the chopped veggies and salted peanuts. Then mix the dressing ingredients and add to the salad. Toss to combine all the ingredients together.

SPRINGY RICE NOODLE SALAD WITH PEA CREAM

This salad always reminds me of one spring when I just couldn't wait for the snow to melt and the sun to finally come out. Fresh dill and pea cream are perfect in a springy salad, and sun-dried tomatoes give a tangy taste. This salad is great for a spring dinner party, or you can make it for yourself on a cold winter day to remind yourself that spring is not far away.

Serves 4–6

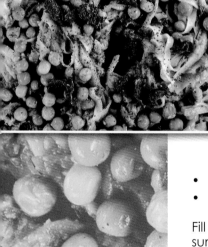

Salad:
- 2–3 Tablespoons sun-dried tomato oil
- 3½ cups sliced white mushrooms
- salt to taste
- 4½ ounces sun-dried tomatoes in oil
- a bunch of fresh dill
- 2–3 Tablespoons soy sauce
- 9 ounces rice noodles
- freshly squeezed lemon juice

Pea cream:
- 14 ounces frozen or fresh green peas
- ½ cup water
- a little bit of ground black pepper
- 2 Tablespoons soy sauce

Fill half of a large pot with water and put it on the boil. Meanwhile, heat sun-dried tomato oil in a pan and add sliced white mushrooms and salt to taste. Cook for a couple of minutes, stirring occasionally. Mix the fried mushrooms, sliced sun-dried tomatoes, chopped fresh dill, and soy sauce in a large salad bowl. Set aside

Prepare the pea cream: leave a handful of peas for the garnish and blend the leftover peas with some water, black pepper, and soy sauce until you get a smooth mixture. Add the pea cream to the salad bowl and mix it with the mushrooms and sun-dried tomatoes.

When the water in the large pot starts to boil, add rice noodles and boil them for about 3 minutes. Drain and rinse with cold water, and add the noodles to the salad bowl. Mix carefully with your hands and garnish with peas and some freshly squeezed lemon juice if you wish. Serve immediately.

LAYERED VEGETABLE SALAD

In Estonia, this salad is actually called "Kasukas," which means "fur-coat," and is usually eaten during the winter season. Such an inappropriate name for a dish in a vegan cookbook! Fortunately my version of this salad contains only super-juicy vegetables, mayo sauce, and scrambled tofu instead of chopped eggs. This festive salad is definitely an eye-catcher on a party table, and if you love beets, this dish is just for you!

Serves 8–10

For the vegetable layers:
- 1¼ cups finely chopped onions
- 2 Tablespoons vinegar
- 3 Tablespoons brown sugar
- ¾ cup hot water
- 1¼ cups finely chopped pickles
- 2½ cups boiled and grated carrots, chilled
- 2 cups boiled and grated potatoes, chilled
- 3 cups boiled and grated beets, chilled

For the mayo sauce:
- 2½ cups vegan mayo
- 2 Tablespoons mild mustard
- salt and ground black pepper to taste

For the scrambled tofu:
- 2 Tablespoons oil
- 1¾ cups crumbled tofu
- ½ teaspoon turmeric
- 1½ teaspoons vegetable stock powder
- ground black pepper to taste
- 3 Tablespoons vegan cream
- 2 teaspoons mild mustard

In a bowl, mix the chopped onions with vinegar, sugar, and hot water. Place the bowl in the fridge and marinate the onions for at least 20 minutes. Prepare the mayo sauce by mixing the mayo with mild mustard and some salt and pepper. Next, heat oil in a pan to prepare the tofu scramble. Add the crumbled tofu to a pan along with turmeric, vegetable stock powder, pepper, vegan cream, and mild mustard. Stir and cook for a couple of minutes. Remove from heat and allow the scrambled tofu to cool. Set aside.

In a big bowl (a transparent bowl would be best to show off the beautiful layers), place some marinated onions for the first layer. Then add a few tablespoons of chopped pickles. Next, add grated potatoes and sprinkle them with salt. Add mayo sauce. Now add the carrot layer and beet layer. Sprinkle them with salt. Add more mayo sauce, and then add another layer of the marinated onions. Continue until you are out of the ingredients. Don't forget to sprinkle salt on almost every other layer. Leave the tofu scramble for the top layer. Let the salad sit in the fridge for at least a couple of hours or overnight before serving it. You can also make the salad into separate little bowls instead of a one big bowl.

PASTA SALAD WITH SUN-DRIED TOMATO PESTO

I just adore this recipe. This salad is rich, filling, and has a lot of flavor. You can use a little bit less garlic if you are not a big fan. Serve it with fresh buns and some lemony mushroom spread if you like.

Serves 4–6

Salad:
- 3½ cups uncooked pasta (farfalle for example)
- 13 ounces black pitted olives
- ½ red onion
- 10 cherry tomatoes

Sun-dried tomato pesto:
- 1 cup sun-dried tomatoes in oil (save the oil)
- 4 handfuls fresh basil
- 4 cloves of garlic
- pinch of ground black pepper
- ½ teaspoon curry powder
- salt to taste, if you are using unsalted sun-dried tomatoes

Cook the pasta *al dente*. Drain it and mix it with olives, sliced red onion, and chopped cherry tomatoes.

Make the pesto: blend sun-dried tomatoes and their oil with basil, garlic, black pepper, and curry powder. Mix the pesto with pasta. Taste and add salt if needed.

CREAMY RICE AND TOFU SALAD WITH SUNFLOWER SEED CREAM

This salad is super creamy with a nice "eggy" texture. It is also really filling since it contains protein-rich tofu and sunflower seed cream. You can add some chopped olives or marinated pickles, if you'd like, but I really like the original recipe. If you are not a big fan of the onions, you can use less or just leave them out.

Serves 6–8

Salad:
- 1½ cups uncooked rice
- 9 ounces firm tofu
- 2 medium onions
- 1½ cups cherry tomatoes, quartered
- fresh dill
- pinch of ground black pepper

Sunflower seed cream:
- 2 cups peeled sunflower seeds
- 1½ cups water
- ½ teaspoon turmeric
- 3 teaspoons vegetable stock powder
- 1 teaspoon lemon juice
- ¼ slice of lemon with peel left on

Soak the sunflower seeds for at least 3 to 4 hours or overnight. You can also boil them for 15 minutes if you are in a hurry. Boil the rice, drain and rinse it, and let it cool down. Crumble the tofu and mix it with rice. Finely chop the onions and mix them with rice and crumbled tofu. Add cherry tomatoes, chopped fresh dill, and ground black pepper.

Now make the cream: drain the soaked or boiled sunflower seeds and put them into a deep bowl. Add all the other ingredients and blend until smooth. Mix the cream with the rice salad. Let the salad sit for a while before serving so the seasoning can really kick in.

CRISPY "FISH" FINGERS

These fellas are crispy on the outside and soft on the inside. They are not identical to real fish fingers but definitely convey a hint of the sea and the creatures that live there. (That didn't sound so appetizing, but these sticks are really delicious.) Serve with vegan mayo and you have a fine appetizer. Or cook some mashed potatoes on the side to have a cozy main dish.

Makes 16 sticks

For the sticks:
- 18 ounces firm tofu

For the marinade:
- 1 Tablespoon lemon juice
- 4 lemon slices, cut in half
- ½ cup oil (use flax seed oil for extra "fishy" flavor)
- 3 Tablespoons dried dill
- ground black pepper to taste
- 4 Tablespoons soy sauce
- ¾ cup hot water
- 1 teaspoon salt
- 3 nori sheets, shredded

For the breading:
- ¾ cup tempura flour
- ½ cup + 2 Tablespoons water
- 1 cup dry breadcrumbs

Cut the tofu into 16 equal sticks. Mix all the marinade ingredients and pour over tofu. Marinate it in the fridge for at least a couple of hours or overnight.

For the breading: mix tempura flour with water. Dip the marinated tofu sticks first into tempura and then roll them in breadcrumbs. Cook on a hot pan at medium heat in plenty of oil until crispy on both sides.

MEATY LENTIL BALLS

I'm very happy with this versatile recipe. You can serve these meaty balls with barbecue sauce as a snack; cook them in tomato sauce and serve with spaghetti; or simmer them in creamy white sauce and serve with mashed potatoes. They hold together really well and taste amazing.

Makes about 40 medium-sized balls

- 1 cup peeled sunflower seeds
- 3 Tablespoons flax meal
- 9 Tablespoons water
- 1 cup uncooked green lentils
- ½ cup uncooked rice
- 2–3 Tablespoons oil
- 1 onion
- ½ teaspoon salt
- ground black pepper to taste
- 4 cloves of garlic
- 1 teaspoon ground nutmeg
- 4 Tablespoons your favorite smoky vegan barbecue sauce
- 2 Tablespoons paprika powder
- 2 teaspoons vegetable stock powder
- ½ cup dry breadcrumbs
- 4 Tablespoons rice flour

Soak the sunflower seeds for a few hours or overnight. Prepare the flax "eggs" by mixing flax meal with water, and leave it in the refrigerator for at least 15 minutes. Boil the lentils and rice together until soft and even a little overcooked.

In the meantime, heat oil in a pan and add chopped onions, salt, and pepper. Cook for about 2 to 3 minutes until golden brown. Add chopped garlic and nutmeg. Cook for about 30 seconds and remove from heat. Drain the lentils and rice very well, so all the liquids will be gone. Also drain and rinse the sunflower seeds and blend them together with barbecue sauce. Mix boiled and drained lentils and rice with fried onion mix. Add paprika powder along with blended sunflower seeds, vegetable stock powder, breadcrumbs, and rice flour. Mix very well.

Preheat the oven to 350°F. Form little balls and cook them in hot oil until crispy. Don't place them on top of each other in a pan but side-by-side, and cook them in 3 to 4 batches. Place the fried lentil balls on a baking tray covered with parchment paper. Cook for 45 minutes at 350°F.

LEMONY MUSHROOM SPREAD

This delightful spread was one of the first recipes I created as a vegan. It has stayed with me ever since. It's tangy, lemony, and really great on a crispy bun. Serve it as an appetizer, and you will surely get some praise from the eaters.

Serves 3–4

- 2 Tablespoons oil
- 5 cups sliced white mushrooms
- ½ teaspoon salt
- ground black pepper to taste
- 1 teaspoon dried thyme
- 1 Tablespoon soy sauce
- ½ slice of lemon with peel left on
- 1 teaspoon grated lemon zest
- 1 teaspoon hard liquor (optional)

Heat oil in a pan. Add sliced mushrooms, salt, pepper, and dried thyme. Cook for about 5 minutes, or until the mushrooms have released their juices. Pour the mushrooms into a bowl and add soy sauce, half a slice of lemon, grated lemon zest, and hard liquor if you wish. Blend until smooth. Taste and add more soy sauce if needed. Let it cool down before serving.

CHEESY ARTICHOKE AND SUN-DRIED TOMATO SPREAD

This spread reminds me a little bit of cottage cheese. It's tangy, cheesy, and just a little sour. I love it! You can serve it with fresh buns or as a dipping sauce with crunchy veggies.

Serves 4–6

- 1½ cups cashews
- 1 (14-ounce) can artichoke hearts
- 3½ ounces sun-dried tomatoes in oil
- 4 Tablespoons sun-dried tomato oil
- ¼ teaspoon ground black pepper

Soak the cashews for at least 3 to 4 hours or overnight. You can also boil them for 15 minutes if you are in a hurry. Drain the soaked cashews and put them into a deep bowl. Add drained artichoke hearts, sun-dried tomatoes, oil, and ground black pepper. Blend until smooth.

BEAN, BROCCOLI, AND PISTACHIO SPREAD

I just adore broccoli and I wanted to use it in a filling spread. I chose white beans as a base and added pistachios for a nutty and salty flavor. The outcome was really nice, and this is perfect served on a fresh bun to accompany a cozy soup.

Serves 4–6

- ¾ cup peeled, salted, and roasted pistachios
- 2 (14-ounce) cans white beans
- 2½ cups chopped fresh broccoli
- 2–3 Tablespoons oil
- 1 teaspoon lemon juice
- ½ teaspoon salt
- a pinch of ground black pepper

Heat 2 to 3 tablespoons of oil in a pan. Add white beans, pistachios, and chopped broccoli. Cook for a couple of minutes. Pour the fried ingredients into a deep bowl and add lemon juice, salt, and ground black pepper. Blend until smooth.

SPICY CASHEW AND BASIL DIP

Cashews are perfect for making anything creamy. If you blend them after soaking, you will have an extra smooth and creamy texture, and you can use it in both savory and sweet dishes. This dip is only one way to use cashews. I like to serve it with fresh and crunchy vegetables.

Serves 4–6

- 1½ cups cashews
- 2–3 handfuls of fresh basil
- 1½ teaspoons curry powder
- ½ teaspoon salt
- ⅔ cup water
- 1½ Tablespoons soy sauce

Soak the cashews for at least 3 to 4 hours or overnight. You can also boil them for 15 minutes if you are in a hurry. Drain and rinse the soaked or boiled cashews and put them into a deep bowl. Add fresh basil, curry powder, salt, water, and soy sauce. Blend until smooth.

BURGERS AND SAVORY PIES

BEAN AND ZUCCHINI CUTLETS

These delicious cutlets have been very popular at my catering events. I created this recipe in the summer when my boyfriend and I were finishing the building of our log cabin. We were really hungry and I happened to find a piece of zucchini and canned beans in our kitchen. And so the recipe was born. I must say these are the best vegan cutlets I have eaten so far. They are chunky, crispy, and juicy, and they kind of remind me the classic cutlets my grandma used to make. I served these fellas as a burger along with fried zucchini slices, red onions, tomatoes, lettuce, vegan mayo, and ketchup sauce.

Makes about 20 medium cutlets

- 2 (14-ounce) cans kidney beans
- 3 bigger onions
- 1 medium zucchini
- 3 teaspoons curry powder
- 3 teaspoons vegetable stock powder
- ¾ cup whole-wheat flour
- oil for cooking

Drain and rinse the beans, put them into a big bowl, and mash them with a fork or your hands (I prefer the last option). Add finely diced onions and zucchini along with curry powder, vegetable stock powder, and whole-wheat flour. Mix carefully with your hands or with a fork. Bring a pan to medium heat and pour a couple of tablespoons of oil in it. Form medium cutlets with your hands and cook them in hot oil until crispy on both sides. Serve with potatoes and gravy, as a burger, or just on bread with a little bit of mild mustard.

EPIC TOFU BURGER WITH HOMEMADE POTATO STRIPS

This burger comes out perfect! It has crispy, breaded tofu; super-juicy, creamy, crunchy salad; spicy mushrooms with a dash of chipotle; and homemade oven-baked potato strips on the side. I was given some tempura flour for Christmas, so I decided to give the breaded tofu a try. The result was really amazing—crispy outside, juicy inside, and very flavorful.

Serves 4–6

For the burger:
- 4–6 burger buns
- 9 ounces firm tofu
- bread crumbs
- a few Tablespoons tempura flour
- your favorite vegan barbecue sauce
- a little bit of salt
- some oil

Prepare tofu the night before by cutting it into 10 medium-sized slices and rubbing the slices with some salt and barbecue sauce. Leave the tofu slices in the fridge to marinate overnight. The next day, mix a few Tablespoons of tempura flour with a little bit of water. Dip the marinated tofu slices into the tempura mix, and then roll them in the bread crumbs. Cook the breaded tofu slices in a hot pan in oil on both sides until golden brown.

For the salad:
- medium iceberg lettuce head
- 2 carrots
- medium-sized piece of root celery
- 1½ cups vegan mayo
- spring onions
- 2 Tablespoons of your favorite vegan barbecue sauce
- soy sauce to taste

Chop the lettuce and mix it with grated carrots, grated root celery, chopped spring onions, mayo, barbecue sauce, and soy sauce.

For the spicy mushrooms:
- oil for cooking
- 3½ cups sliced white mushrooms
- salt to taste
- chipotle pepper powder to taste

Heat oil in a pan. Add mushroom slices, salt, and chipotle pepper powder. Cook for a couple of minutes, stirring occasionally.

For the oven-baked potato strips:
- 10–15 medium potatoes
- 3–4 Tablespoons oil
- salt to taste
- some spicy tomato sauce for serving

Preheat the oven to 440°F. Wash and peel the potatoes, cut them into strips, and put them into a big bowl. Add salt and oil and use your hands to mix the potatoes, oil, and salt together. Pour the potatoes on a baking tray covered with parchment paper and cook them for about 35 minutes until golden brown and crispy.

To make a burger, spread some salad on a roll, add two slices of breaded tofu and mushrooms, and then place the other roll on the top. Serve with potato strips and your favorite spicy tomato sauce.

SPLIT PEA BURGERS

These crispy and golden pea patties have been my one of my favorite recipes for years. They are very tasty, super cheap, and easy to make. I love to serve them at parties, and when I have to make a lot of burgers, I always use this recipe. When the patties do not want to stick together (it almost never happens, but even patties can have a bad day), then add some flour (almost any flour will do).

Serves 8–10

For the pea patties:
- 1 ⅓ cups dried yellow split peas (or any other type of pea you like)
- 3–4 Tablespoons oil
- 2–4 onions, chopped
- soy sauce to taste
- vegetable stock powder to taste
- curry powder to taste
- about ½ cup water
- oil for cooking

Soak the peas overnight. Heat oil in a pan, and sauté the onions until golden brown, adding soy sauce to taste. Drain, rinse, and pour the soaked peas into a bowl or food processor. Add fried onions, vegetable stock powder, curry powder, and water (I used a lot of curry powder, about 4 Tablespoons). Taste the mixture and add more stock powder, curry powder, or soy sauce if you wish. Crush the peas with a food processor or a hand blender until the mixture is really smooth and not grainy. It will be pretty wet but don't hesitate. Heat oil (I used plenty) in a cooking pan, form the patties, and cook in hot oil until crispy on both sides. The patties are best on the same day; they tend to get dry over time.

For the burger sauce:
- vegan mayo
- some quality ketchup
- dried oregano
- some salt and pepper to taste

Mix all the ingredients. Serve the burger with pea patties, sauce, and your favorite fillings (I mostly like to add sliced onions and pickles).

BEET AND BEAN PATTIES

I'm a huge beet fan! I like them roasted in soups, salads, and spreads. And the beets definitely shine in this dish. These patties are so beautiful with their deep red color, and you can serve them in a burger or as a side with mashed potatoes and gravy. When I'm making patties, I almost always like to make big batches of them. Feel free to cut the ingredients in half if you don't want so many patties.

Serves 10–12

- 3 cups dried fava beans
- 4 boiled beets, chopped
- 2–3 Tablespoons whole-wheat flour
- 2–3 Tablespoons rice porridge or the same amount of any kind of flour
- 1 onion, chopped
- 2 teaspoons ground cumin
- 2–3 Tablespoons curry powder
- vegetable stock powder to taste

Soak the beans overnight. Drain and rinse. Use a hand blender, food processor, or mince meat machine to grind all the ingredients until smooth and mixed well together. Taste and add more spices, herbs, or vegetable stock powder. Form the patties and cook in a pan in hot oil until crispy on both sides. Make sure there is enough oil and that it is hot before putting the patties in it. One side of the patty has to be completely cooked before you try to turn it over in a pan. Use a very thin pan spade for the turning. The patties are best if you let them cool down a little before eating.

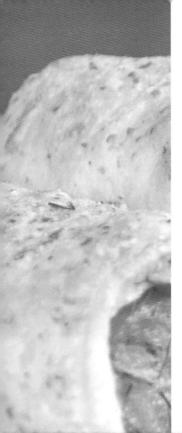

CARROTS IN A BLANKET

I wish pigs in a blanket were actually cute pigs in a warm blanket instead of sausages made out of actual pigs. But who needs sausages when you have delicious, juicy, and vibrant carrots? I must be honest and confess that this recipe idea was actually created by my boyfriend. We were visiting our vegetarian friends, and we had a pack of puff pastry and a bunch of carrots. I just **love** recipes like these—so simple, cheap, and delicious in their simplicity. Carrots really shine in this dish. Add fresh dill to the filling, and before you know you'll have eaten at least four of those cute little pies!

Makes about 24 pies

- 12 medium carrots
- 17 ⅓ ounces frozen vegan puff pastry
- handful of fresh dill
- salt and pepper to taste
- oil for cooking

Take the puff pastry out of the freezer and put it in a regular fridge for at least a couple of hours or overnight before baking. Wash the carrots, cut them in half, and boil them until soft. Drain and let them cool. Peel them, heat oil in a pan, and cook the carrots until golden brown. Add some salt and pepper to taste. I cooked the carrots in two batches because I had so many.

Mix the carrots with chopped fresh dill. Preheat the oven to 430°F. Roll out the puff pastry on a floured surface. Cut out 24 squares and roll a carrot into every square. Cover the baking tray with parchment paper and put the pies on it. Bake for 15 minutes. Serve as a snack or with soup.

LENTIL AND VEGETABLE PIE

This pie has become quite legendary in my kitchen. I usually bake it for different parties and people really love it. It is filling, hearty, tasty, and comforting. And it tastes really delicious even the next day. The "secret" ingredients in this pie are definitely curry powder and pickles.

Makes 20–25 square pieces

For the yeast dough:
- 2 Tablespoons active dry yeast
- ½ teaspoon salt
- ½ teaspoon dried thyme
- 2½ cups all-purpose flour
- 1 cup + 1 Tablespoon lukewarm water
- 2 Tablespoons oil

Mix the dry ingredients (yeast, salt, thyme, and flour). Add water. Mix with your hands a little bit and then add the oil. Mix again and knead hard on a floured surface until the dough is elastic. Put the dough ball into a bowl and cover the bowl with a clean kitchen towel. Leave it in a warm place to rise for 30 to 45 minutes. In the meantime you can prepare the filling.

For the filling:
- 1 ⅓ cups uncooked green lentils
- 2 Tablespoons oil
- 2 onions
- 1 large zucchini
- 2 cloves of garlic
- 1–2 Tablespoons curry powder
- 1 tomato
- 2–3 pickles
- vegetable stock powder, salt, and/or soy sauce to taste
- ¾ cups tomato juice

Boil the lentils until soft. In the meantime, heat oil in a pan and add chopped onions. Cook until golden brown. Add grated zucchini, chopped garlic, curry powder, chopped tomato, chopped pickles, and vegetable stock powder, salt, and/or soy sauce to taste. Cook for 5 minutes. Add tomato juice and simmer until the lentils are boiling. Drain the lentils and add them to the filling. Stir and taste. Add seasoning if needed. Simmer until there's not a lot of liquid left.

Preheat the oven to 400°F. Put the raised dough on a floured surface, knead for a couple of minutes, and then roll it wider. Spread some oil on a baking tray and put the rolled dough on it. Lengthen the dough edges so the dough is covering the whole baking tray. Let the dough rise in a warm place for about 10 to 15 minutes.

Spread the filling on the raised dough and bake the pie for about 25 to 30 minutes. Let it cool for about 10 minutes before cutting it.

PUFF PASTRY TRIANGLES

These yummy little pies are super soft and filled with a flavorful and rich carrot, rice, and sun-dried tomato mixture. They are pretty easy to make and also perfect to grab as a quick snack for work or school.

Makes 24 triangles

- 17 1/3 ounces frozen vegan puff pastry
- 1/2 cup rice, cooked
- 1 cup chopped sun-dried tomatoes in oil
- 2 cups boiled carrots mashed with a fork
- 1 onion
- 1/4 teaspoon dried thyme
- 2 Tablespoons sun-dried tomato oil
- 2–2 1/2 teaspoons salt

Place the frozen dough into the refrigerator for a few hours or the night before you intend to bake it. The next day, unfold the pastry on a lightly floured surface. Roll it thinner and cut into 24 squares. Mix together the rest of the ingredients to make the filling. Place 2 to 3 tablespoons of filling onto the center of each square. Fold pastry end over to form a triangle. Crimp edges to seal. Place on a baking tray covered with parchment paper. Bake at 400°F until the triangles puff up high and are nicely browned. If you have some leftover filling, you can add it to a pattie mixture or just eat it on a bread.

MAIN DISHES

SAVORY FILLED PANCAKES

Many years ago I went to a birthday party where the hostess made lovely, savory filled pancakes and a big pot of borscht soup. For me, this was an ideal birthday dish. I just love hearty and homemade meals made with love. Actually, pancakes made this way are called **Komm Morgen wieder**, meaning "Come back tomorrow," because the filling is usually made with leftover beef. But of course no animals are ever harmed in my recipes. I really wanted to have a vegan version of this dish and it turned out amazing! I made a juicy spinach and chickpea filling, but I have also tried mince soy mixed with barbecue sauce. Folding these pancakes may seem tricky at first, but you will master it very soon and then it will be rather easy. And if you don't have time to fold the pancake envelopes, just serve the pancakes and the filling separately.

Makes about 10–11 pancakes

For the batter:
- 2½ cups all-purpose flour
- 1 teaspoon baking soda
- 1 teaspoon baking powder
- ½ teaspoon salt
- 2 teaspoons vinegar
- 2¾ cups water

Mix the flour with baking soda, baking powder, and salt. Add water and vinegar. Mix well (I whisked). Leave the batter to rest until you prepare the filling.

For the filling:
- 2 Tablespoons oil
- 14 ounces frozen spinach
- ½ cup water
- 2 (14-ounce) cans chickpeas
- ½ teaspoon salt
- 4 Tablespoons vegan cream
- 2 Tablespoons soy sauce
- ½ teaspoon curry powder

Heat oil in a pan and add frozen spinach and water. Simmer for 2 to 3 minutes. Add canned chickpeas, salt, vegan cream, soy sauce, and curry powder. Mix and cook for a couple of minutes. Set the filling aside.

For the mayo sauce:
- ¾ cup vegan mayo
- 1 teaspoon ground paprika
- ½ teaspoon curry powder
- ½ Tablespoon soy sauce

Mix all the ingredients.

Now it's time to start baking the pancakes. First of all, take two big plates, grease them, and set aside. Now heat the pan, add oil (not too much), pour the batter onto the pan, and cook on one side until golden brown. Now take the half-baked pancake and put it carefully on one of the greased plates with the uncooked (yes, uncooked!) side facing down. Add about 2 tablespoons of filling onto the center of each pancake. Fold the pancake edges onto the filling like an envelope. Put all the filled and folded pancakes onto the other greased plate. When all the pancakes are prepared this way (half-baked, filled, and folded), bake them again in hot oil until the uncooked sides are completely cooked and golden brown. Serve with mayo sauce.

BEAN PILAF

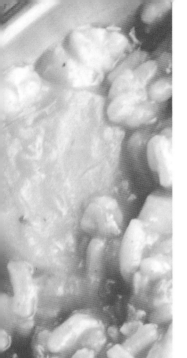

Have I told you about the importance of bay leaves? They have been very underrated in my kitchen. I decided to correct that mistake and cook a tasty pilaf with some protein-rich beans and flavorful bay leaves. I actually make this dish quite often because I almost always have the ingredients at home, it is rather cheap, and everyone always loves it.

Serves 4–6

- 3 Tablespoons oil
- 1 large onion
- 1 large carrot
- 3 garlic cloves
- 3 handfuls of rice
- 1 (14-ounce) can kidney beans
- 2–3 bay leaves
- a pinch of ground black pepper
- 2 teaspoons vegetable stock powder
- 1 teaspoon brown sugar
- 1 cup tomato juice
- 3 Tablespoons your favorite vegan barbecue sauce
- 2 Tablespoons vegan cream (optional)
- fresh parsley for garnish

Put a thick-bottomed pot on a stove and heat the oil. Add chopped onions and carrot. Cook for a couple of minutes, stirring from time to time. Add chopped garlic cloves and rice, and pour enough water on it so there are a few inches of water above the rice. Add drained and rinsed kidney beans, bay leaves, pepper, vegetable stock powder, and brown sugar. Stir and boil on medium heat under the lid until the rice is soft. Add the tomato juice and the barbecue sauce and stir. You can also add some vegan cream if you want the dish to be a little bit creamier. Garnish with fresh parsley.

CRISPY OVEN-BAKED SPRING ROLLS

I have a major problem with deep frying food. First of all, it's a waste of oil; second, it is unhealthy; and third, it's a lot of mess! But I had a craving for delicious homemade spring rolls, so I decided to bake them instead. The result was pretty amazing! The rolls were juicy on the inside and crispy on the outside. I served them with some quality store-bought sweet chili sauce and basmati rice with peanut butter sauce on the side.

Makes about 26 spring rolls

- 1–2 inches ginger root
- 2 carrots
- 21 ounces head cabbage
- 4 Tablespoons oil
- 3 big garlic gloves
- 3½ cups chopped white mushrooms
- 3–4 Tablespoons soy sauce
- 6–7 sheets of phyllo dough (put it in the regular fridge the night before)
- oil to spread on the rolls before baking

Peel and grate the ginger and carrots. Finely chop the head cabbage. Set aside ginger, carrots, and cabbage. Heat oil in a large pan (wok, for example) and add crushed garlic cloves and grated ginger. Cook for about 10 seconds and then add grated carrots. Cook for a few minutes and then add chopped head cabbage. Stir and cook for about 5 minutes. Finely chop the mushrooms and add to the pan. Stir, cover with a lid, and let it simmer on the same heat for 10 to 15 minutes. Add a little bit of water if needed. Finally, season the filling with soy sauce.

Preheat the oven to 480°F. Take the phyllo dough from the fridge. Place one phyllo sheet on a wide cutting board and cut it into 4 squares. Add one tablespoon of filling on the left, bottom corner. Roll the corner onto the filling and keep rolling until you reach the middle of the square. Then turn the left and right corners onto the middle and keep rolling until you reach the end. Repeat the procedure until you are out of the filling. Cover the baking tray with parchment paper and place the spring rolls on it. Bake the rolls for 5 minutes at 480°F, then turn the heat down to 440°F and bake for 10 minutes until golden brown.

SPINACH AND GREEN BEAN LASAGNA

I have tried so many different versions of vegan lasagna in my life. Even lasagna with a buckwheat filling has been on my menu (pretty weird, I know). I was really craving lasagna filled with juicy spinach and green beans, so I created one. I had guests over, and they ate every piece and even scraped the baking dish clean!

Serves 4–6

For the sunflower seed cream:
- 1 cup peeled sunflower seeds
- 1 teaspoon vegetable stock powder
- ¾ cup water

For the filling:
- 2 Tablespoons oil
- 14 ounces frozen spinach
- 14 ounces frozen green beans
- ½ cup water
- 1 teaspoon salt
- pinch of ground black pepper
- 3 Tablespoons soy sauce
- 24 lasagna sheets

For the sauce:
- 4 cups tomato juice
- pinch of ground black pepper
- ½ cup vegan cream
- 1 teaspoon salt
- 2 Tablespoons brown sugar

Soak the sunflower seeds a few hours or boil them for 15 minutes if you are in a hurry. Drain and rinse the soaked or boiled seeds and move to a deep bowl. Add vegetable stock powder and water. Blend until you have a smooth cream. Set aside.

For the filling, heat oil in a pan. Add frozen spinach, green beans, water, salt, pepper, and soy sauce. Simmer for 10 to 15 minutes.

For the sauce, mix all the ingredients in a pot, boil for a couple of minutes, and set aside.

Now start assembling the lasagna. Grease a deep 12 x 9 inch baking dish. Place 6 lasagna sheets onto the bottom (I put 4 lengthwise and 2 widthwise). Add one-third of the filling and then spread about 3 Tablespoons of sunflower seed cream evenly onto the filling. Add a scoop of the sauce and then add another 6 lasagna sheets. Make two more layers. For the last layer, place the last 6 lasagna sheets onto the top. Add all the remaining tomato sauce and spread the remaining sunflower seed cream evenly onto the sheets. Bake the lasagna at 400°F for 45 minutes or until the sheets are soft. If the lasagna looks like it's getting too dry on the top, cover the dish with foil. Let sit for 10 minutes before serving.

CREAMY CHILI BEAN AND ZUCCHINI STEW

The first time I made this spicy and creamy stew, my boyfriend and I were in our log cabin. It was a lovely summer day and my mom had sent me a bunch of zucchini she had grown. I also had some chili beans (I almost always have some, they are great!) and some vegan cream. So I made this juicy stew and we ate it with pasta. This is also great on a party table or at family get-togethers. It is pretty spicy yet super delicious. You can use regular canned beans instead of chili beans to make it more kid-friendly. Serve it with rice, pasta, or potatoes.

Serves 4–6

- 2–3 Tablespoons oil
- 2 onions
- 1 teaspoon salt
- pinch of ground black pepper
- 1 large zucchini, sliced
- 1 cup water
- 2 (14-ounce) cans beans in chili sauce
- 1 cup vegan cream
- 1 teaspoon grated lemon zest
- 2 teaspoons vegetable stock powder
- 1 Tablespoon soy sauce (optional)

Heat oil in a thick-bottomed pot, and add chopped onions, salt, and pepper. Cook for about 2 minutes until golden brown. Add sliced zucchini and cook for about a minute. Add water, beans, cream, lemon zest, and vegetable stock powder. Boil on medium heat for about 15 minutes. Taste and add soy sauce if desired.

HEAVENLY CABBAGE ROLLS

I have finally decided that these cabbage rolls are my favorite food on Earth. It may change, but right now I just can't get enough of them. They're not the easiest to prepare, but they are definitely worth the work. I get so excited every time I make them, and each roll is a little piece of heaven. Simply serve with boiled potatoes and you have an amazing home-style main dish.

Makes 10–11 cabbage rolls

For the rolls:
- whole head cabbage (about 5 ½ pounds)
- 2 cups dry soy mince
- ½ cup rice, uncooked
- 3 Tablespoons oil
- 2 medium onions
- ½–1 teaspoon salt
- ground black pepper to taste
- ¼ teaspoon ground nutmeg
- 2 Tablespoons rice flour
- 3–4 Tablespoons soy sauce

For the sauce:
- 3 cups tomato juice
- 1 cup vegan cream
- ground black pepper to taste
- 2 Tablespoons brown sugar
- 1 teaspoon salt

Carefully cut out the core from the cabbage head. Place whole head into a large pot, cover with water, and boil under the lid until the cabbage leaves are softened enough to pull off individual leaves. Carefully drain the cabbage head and rinse with cold water. Very carefully remove the leaves (you will need about 10 to 11 leaves). With a small and sharp knife, cut away the thick center stem from each leaf, without cutting all the way through. You can use the remaining cabbage in stews, soups, or casseroles.

Now prepare the filling. Boil soy mince and rice together, until slightly overcooked. Drain until you have no liquids left. Heat up 3 tablespoons of oil in a pan and add finely chopped onions, salt, pepper, and nutmeg. Cook until the onions are golden brown. Add the drained rice and soy mixture. Stir and cook for a couple of minutes. Add rice flour and soy sauce. Stir and remove the heat.

Prepare the sauce. In a smaller pot, mix tomato juice, vegan cream, black pepper, brown sugar, and salt. Boil for a couple of minutes.

Preheat the oven to 400°F and start preparing the rolls. Place 1 to 2 tablespoons of filling onto the center of each cabbage leaf. Flip the right side of the leaf to the middle, then flip the left side. Now roll away from you until you have a nice and firm cabbage roll. Continue the procedure until you have 10 to 11 cabbage rolls. Grease a deep baking pan and place the rolls into the pan. Bake for 1 hour until golden brown. Then pour the sauce onto the rolls and bake for 10 more minutes. Serve with boiled potatoes.

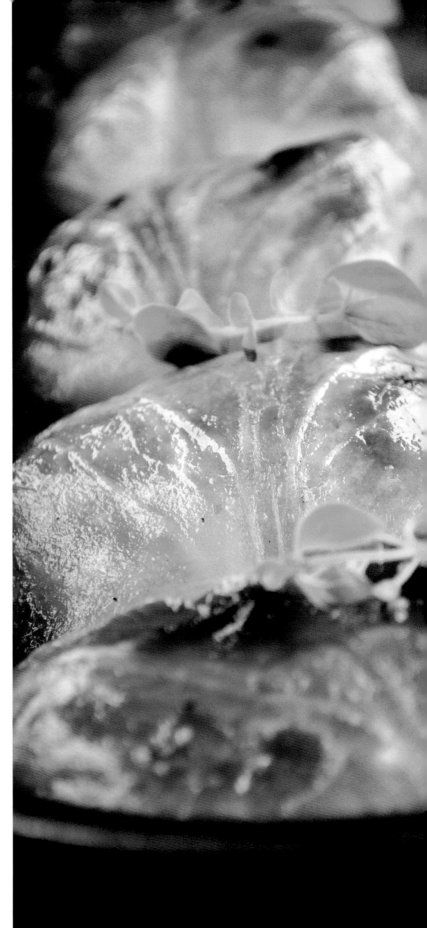

SHEPHERD'S PIE

I have tried many shepherd's pie recipes, and I was never satisfied until I finally created this one. The filling is a little bit spicy and smoky. Lentils and mushrooms make it meatier, and pickles give a little juicy crunch. You can leave out the mushrooms if you're not a fan. Serve hot with mild mustard sauce for example.

Serves 8–10

For the mash:
- 2¼ pounds potatoes
- 3 medium carrots
- ½ cup vegan cream
- ¼ cup warm water
- 1 teaspoon salt

Wash and peel the potatoes and carrots. Chop the potatoes into large chunks and slice the carrots into coins. Boil the potatoes and carrots together until completely soft. Drain and put them back into the same pot. Add cream, water, and salt. Mash until smooth. Set aside while you make the filling.

For the filling:
- 1 cup uncooked green lentils
- 3 Tablespoons oil
- 2 onions
- pinch of salt
- 2 celery ribs
- 3½ cups chopped white mushrooms
- 2 tomatoes
- 4 pickles
- 2 cups tomato juice
- 3 Tablespoons your favorite smoky vegan barbecue sauce
- 2½ teaspoons vegetable stock powder
- 1 teaspoon curry powder
- 1 Tablespoon brown sugar

Boil the lentils until soft (don't add salt while boiling). Drain and set aside. Preheat the oven to 400°F. Heat oil in a large pan. Add chopped onions and a pinch of salt. Cook for a couple of minutes and add finely sliced celery ribs. Cook for a minute. Add chopped white mushrooms and cook for a couple of minutes until the mushrooms have released their juices. Add chopped tomatoes and pickles along with tomato juice, barbecue sauce, vegetable stock powder, curry powder, and brown sugar. Simmer for 5 to 7 minutes. Grease a medium-sized deep baking dish and pour in the filling. Now spread the mashed potatoes evenly on top (I used a spatula and a fork). Bake for 40 minutes. Garnish with fresh herbs.

MEATY LENTIL BALL SAUCE

My mom used to make this sauce with meatballs when I wasn't a vegan yet. I loved it, and now I am happy to present you my vegan version of it. It's almost identical to the original recipe. The balls are meaty in the creamy sauce, and it goes perfectly with potatoes—a really hearty main dish.

Serves 4–6

- 3 Tablespoons oil
- 1 onion
- ½ teaspoon salt
- pinch of ground black pepper
- ½ teaspoon ground nutmeg
- ½ cup all-purpose flour
- 4½ cups hot water
- 1 Tablespoon dried dill
- ½ Tablespoon vegetable stock powder
- 1–2 Tablespoons soy sauce
- ½ cup vegan cream
- 15–17 Meaty Lentil Balls (see page 22)

Heat oil in a thick-bottomed pot. Add chopped onions, salt, pepper, and ground nutmeg. Cook for a couple of minutes. Add flour and stir with a fork for about 30 seconds. Now add water and stir very well. Add dried dill, vegetable stock powder, soy sauce, and cream. Stir and simmer on medium heat for 5 minutes. Add lentil balls, stir, bring to a boil, and remove from heat.

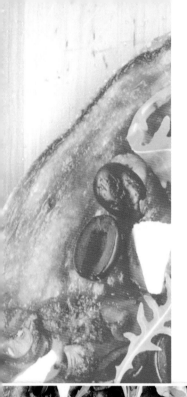

VEGGIE PIZZA WITH CRISPY THIN CRUST

My boyfriend really wanted pizza with a thin and crispy crust. I'm also a fan of thin crusts, but I never thought it would be *that* easy to make it at home. In fact, all you need is flour and water. No yeast, no fuss. And you can use your favorite veggies, mushrooms, and whatnot for the toppings. I love olives, so I added a lot of them. Feel free to leave them out or replace them with something else if you're not a fan.

Makes 2 large 14-inch pizzas

For the crust:
- 2 cups all-purpose flour
- 1 cup whole-wheat flour
- ½ teaspoon salt
- ½ teaspoon dried thyme
- 2 Tablespoons oil
- 1 cup hot water

Preheat the oven to 480°F. In a large bowl, mix flours with salt and thyme. Add oil and mix it with flour using your fingers. Add half of the water, mix, add the remaining half, and mix with your hands until you get a dough ball. When the dough ball doesn't stick to your fingers anymore, put it in the plastic wrap and let it sit for 10 minutes. In the meantime you can prepare the toppings.

For the toppings:
- 4 Tablespoons oil
- 3½ cups sliced white mushrooms
- ½ teaspoon salt
- pinch of ground black pepper
- medium head of broccoli
- 12 Tablespoons quality ketchup or tomato sauce
- 2½ cups black pitted olives
- 1¼ cups canned pineapple chunks
- couple of handfuls of fresh arugula

Heat 2 Tablespoons of oil in a pan. Add sliced mushrooms, salt, and pepper. Cook for a few minutes until the mushrooms have released their juices.

Add chopped broccoli and cook for a couple of minutes. Now add 4 Tablespoons of the ketchup or tomato sauce, stir, and cook for a minute. Remove from heat.

Preheat oven to 480°F. Put the dough ball on a floured surface. Cut it into two equal halves. Roll one half into a large thin round (about 14 inches) and put it carefully on a baking tray covered with parchment paper. Now spread the other 2 Tablespoons of oil onto the dough (prevents tomato paste from soaking into the crust), and then spread 4 Tablespoons of ketchup or tomato sauce onto the dough. Add half of the mushroom and broccoli topping and spread it evenly onto the pizza. Add half of the olives (I cut them in half lengthwise) and half of the pineapple chunks. Follow the same procedure with the other pizza. Now you have two large pizzas on a baking tray waiting to get in the oven. Put one pizza in the hot oven and bake it for 10 minutes. Remove from oven and garnish with fresh arugula. Now bake the other pizza. Serve immediately.

CREAMY CARROT AND ZUCCHINI PASTA

I made this pasta for brunch for some of my dear friends. They had only good things to say about it, and one of them thought it was made with eggs, as sunflower seeds really give such an "eggy" and super-filling texture to everything. Zucchini will make it juicy, and carrots give it a little crunch.

Serves 4–6

For the sunflower seed cream:
- 2 cups peeled sunflower seeds
- 2½ teaspoons vegetable stock powder
- 1 teaspoon lemon juice
- 1½ cups water

For the carrot and zucchini mix:
- 2–3 Tablespoons oil
- 1 onion
- salt and pepper to taste
- 3 cloves of garlic
- 2½ cups grated carrots
- 4 cups grated zucchini
- 2 Tablespoons soy sauce
- 3 cups uncooked pasta (*fusilli tricolore* for example)

Soak the sunflower seeds at least 3 to 4 hours or overnight. You can also boil them for 15 minutes if you are in a hurry. Drain the soaked seeds and move into a deep bowl. Add vegetable stock powder, lemon juice, and water. Blend until smooth.

Heat oil in a thick-bottomed pot. Add chopped onions, salt, and pepper. Cook for a couple of minutes. Add garlic and cook for another 30 seconds. Add grated carrots, cook for a couple of minutes, and then add grated zucchini. Cook for 3 to 4 minutes. Add sunflower seed cream and soy sauce. Stir and cook for about a minute. Serve with pasta cooked *al dente*.

PIEROGI WITH MY FAVORITE GARLIC SAUCE

Pierogi are filled dumplings, and they originate from Central and Eastern Europe. I like to make them quite often, since you only need flour and water for the dough and you can use almost any leftovers for the filling. But since this is still a dinner party book, I made the filling extra tasty and the sauce heavenly. If you are a fan of garlic, this sauce will knock your socks off!

Serves 4–6

For the dough:
- 3 cups all-purpose flour
- 1 cup water
- 2 Tablespoons oil

Mix the flour with oil and massage it in with your fingers. Add half of the water, mix, add the remaining half, and mix with your hands until you get a dough ball. When the dough ball doesn't stick to your fingers anymore, put it in the plastic wrap and let it sit until you prepare the filling.

For the mashed veggies:
- 1 pound root veggies (for example 2 potatoes, carrot, piece of root celery, and turnip)
- ½ cup vegan cream
- salt and ground black pepper to taste

Wash and peel the veggies. Cut into large chunks and boil until completely soft. Drain, add cream, and mash until smooth. Add salt and pepper to taste. Mix and taste for salt.

For the garlic sauce:
- 5 cloves of garlic
- ½ cup quality cold-pressed oil
- ¼ cup soy sauce

Crush the garlic and mix it with oil and soy sauce. Whisk until smooth.

Begin filling the pierogi. Take a little bit of dough, form a little ball, and roll it into a circle. Add about 1 teaspoon of filling, pinch the edges together with your fingers, and then use a fork to close them. Put the filled pierogi on a floured surface—don't place them on top of each other or they will stick. Boil the fresh pierogi for about 8 to 10 minutes in plenty of water. Drain very carefully and serve immediately with garlic sauce. You can also pan-fry or bake them instead of boiling.

QUICK BOLOGNESE

I always have some dry soy mince and tomato juice on hand. They are really useful if you have unexpected guests or if you are just really hungry and want to make a quick and filling vegan dish like this Bolognese—a really effortless yet very tasty dinner!

Serves 4–6

- 3 Tablespoons oil
- 2 onions
- ½ teaspoon salt
- ground black pepper to taste
- 4 cloves of garlic
- 2 cups dry soy mince
- 1 Tablespoon brown sugar
- ¼ teaspoon dried thyme
- 3 cups tomato juice

Heat oil in a pan. Add chopped onions, salt, and pepper. Cook for a couple of minutes until golden brown. Add chopped garlic and cook for 30 seconds. Add soy mince, sugar, thyme, and tomato juice. Simmer for 5 minutes until the soy granules are soft. Garnish with fresh basil and serve with spaghetti.

CREAMY GARLICKY POTATOES AND BEANS

In the town near my parents' home, there's a really cozy tavern. They have this amazing dish on the menu—creamy garlicky potatoes. When I went to high school, my classmate's mom was working as a cook there and I just had to ask for the recipe for this dish. They use light cream in their version, but I substituted it with vegan cream. I also added some beans to make it more filling. These potatoes work nicely as a main or side dish.

Serves 3–4

- 2–3 Tablespoons oil
- 8 potatoes, boiled
- salt and pepper to taste
- 14-ounce can red kidney beans
- 3 garlic gloves
- a little bit of fresh dill
- 3 Tablespoons vegan cream
- soy sauce to taste

Heat oil in a large pan. Add sliced, boiled potatoes and cook until golden brown. Add some salt and pepper. Add drained beans, chopped garlic, fresh dill, and vegan cream. Stir well, add soy sauce to taste, and serve immediately.

CAULIFLOWER AND TOFU CURRY

What's not to love about cauliflower? I bake it in the oven with rye bread crumbs or throw it into soups, stews, and salads. I even add it to mashed potatoes. Cauliflower is definitely a star in this delicious curry recipe. It has a vibrant yellow color, and it is mellow rather than spicy. I cut the tofu into bigger cubes, because I really wanted this curry to be chunky. Serve it with rice noodles or boiled rice.

Serves 4–6

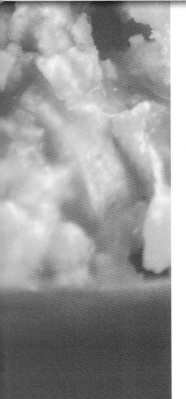

- 3 Tablespoons oil
- 9 ounces firm tofu
- 1-inch piece ginger root, chopped
- ½ teaspoon turmeric
- ¼ teaspoon ground cumin
- 1 teaspoon curry powder
- 2 bay leaves
- 4 cups cauliflower, chopped
- 1½ cups coconut milk
- 1 teaspoon salt

Heat oil in a thick-bottomed pot. Add tofu cubes and cook until crispy and slightly golden brown. Add chopped ginger root, turmeric, cumin, curry powder, and bay leaves. Stir and cook for about a minute. Add chopped cauliflower and cook for about 30 seconds. Now add coconut milk and salt. Boil on medium heat covered for about 15 minutes. Serve with rice noodles or boiled rice.

BAKED ONIONS WITH CREAMY LEMONY MUSHROOM FILLING

The first time I made filled and baked onions was a couple of years ago at Christmas. These onions were definitely a hit! This time the filling came out extra tasty. Creamy and lemony and also containing my favorite sunflower seed cream. And the filling also contains raisins! Weird, I know, but they fit just perfectly, trust me. You can leave the raisons out if you're not a fan. The cooking time for this dish is about one and a half hours, but it's totally worth it. A perfect main dish!

Makes 8 filled onions

For the onions and filling:
- 8 onions (any type of onion is fine)
- 2 Tablespoons oil
- 3½ cups sliced white mushrooms
- 2 round lemon slices with peel left on
- 2 handfuls of raisins (soak them in hot water for a couple of minutes)
- 2 Tablespoons fresh lemon juice
- salt and pepper to taste
- a little bit of oil

For the cream:
- 1 cup peeled sunflower seeds (soak them for 3–4 hours or boil 15 minutes)
- ¾ cups water
- 1 teaspoon vegetable stock powder
- a handful of fresh dill

Bring a big pot of water to boil. Add onions (leave the peel on!) and boil them for 15 minutes until almost soft. Carefully drain the onions and rinse them with cold water. Cut off the top of each onion and peel. Use a small sharp knife to remove the center of each onion, keeping about 2 layers of the onion. If there's a hole in the bottom of an onion, cover it with a small onion slice. Put the onions on a greased baking pan and prepare the filling.

Preheat the oven to 400°F. Take about a handful of scooped out onion centers (you can use the leftover centers to make different soups, sauces, and spreads) and chop them finely. Heat up a pan, add oil, and cook the chopped onions until slightly golden. Add finely chopped mushrooms and cook for about 5 minutes. Add chopped lemon slices and some salt and pepper to taste.

Prepare the cream: drain the soaked or boiled sunflower seeds and mix them with water, vegetable stock powder, and fresh dill. Blend until smooth. Add the cream and soaked and drained raisins to the mushrooms. Add some salt if needed. Mix carefully and fill the onions using a teaspoon. Brush every onion with a little bit of oil. Bake for 35 minutes. Serve with mashed potatoes and gravy or with rice, buckwheat, and fresh salad.

NO-BAKE DESSERTS

DREAMY CHOCOLATE AND CHERRY CAKE

This is it. This is the real deal. This cake is the most moist, creamy, delicious cake ever. I have to thank my friend René for the inspiration. This recipe uses coconut whipped cream, which you can easily make at home. I have to warn you though that there is a tremendous risk of eating the whole cake by yourself!

Note: Before making this cake, ensure that the coconut milk cans have been in the fridge overnight.

Makes one 11-inch cake

For the crust:
- 10½ ounces vegan cookies ("digestive" for example)
- 5 ounces vegan margarine

Crush the cookies and mix them with melted margarine. Take a round cake pan (11 inches) and put it on a baking sheet. Draw out the round, cut it out, and put it onto the bottom of an oiled cake pan. Pour the cookie and margarine mixture into the cake pan and push it evenly onto the bottom. Cover the pan with a plastic wrap and put it in the fridge for at least half an hour.

For the topping:
- 7 ounces dark vegan chocolate
- 2 (14-ounce) cans coconut milk (full fat)
- 3–4 Tablespoons sugar
- 3 Tablespoons cocoa powder
- 2 teaspoons agar-agar powder
- 21 ounces canned pitted cherries
- crushed almonds

Melt the chocolate in a water bath and leave it to cool down to room temperature. In the meantime, take the coconut milk cans out of the fridge and flip them upside down. Open the cans and pour away the liquid or keep it for some other dish. Scoop the hardened coconut cream out of the cans into a deep bowl, add sugar and cocoa powder, and whip with a hand mixer until fluffy. Pour in the cooled-down and melted chocolate and whip some more. Now, in a saucepan, mix the agar-agar powder with a couple of Tablespoons of cold water and bring the mixture to boil while stirring fast. When it starts to boil, stir for about 10 seconds, and then remove from heat and let the mixture cool down for about a minute. If it's a little lumpy, mix it with a hand mixer. Add the agar-agar mixture to the whipped cream and whip it again until everything is mixed.

Take the crust out of the fridge. Drain the cherries and add evenly to the crust. Now scoop the whipped mixture onto the crust and cherries and spread it out evenly. Add crushed almonds, cover the cake pan with a plastic wrap, and put it back in the fridge for a few hours (overnight would be best) before serving.

ESTONIAN COOKIE CAKE

This layered cookie cake is very popular in Estonia. Every family has their own recipe, and different kinds of cookies, berries, and cream are used. I made my own version containing bananas and coconut whipped cream. This cake is so simple that even little kids can do it. It is definitely best served the next day or even the day after. You can use any seasonal berries or fruit of your choice.

Note: Before making this cake, ensure that the coconut milk cans have been in the fridge overnight.

Serves 6–8

- 3 (14-ounce) cans coconut milk (full fat)
- 2 Tablespoons vanilla sugar
- 2½ Tablespoons sugar
- 2 teaspoons grated lemon zest
- 12 ⅓ ounces square vegan cookies (4 layers of 12 cookies)
- plant milk or juice for dipping the cookies (I used soy milk.)
- 4–5 bananas
- berries of your choice for garnishing

Take the coconut milk cans out of the fridge and flip them upside down. Open the cans and pour away the liquid or keep it for some other dish. Scoop the hardened coconut cream out of the cans into a deep bowl and add sugars and lemon zest. Whip with a hand mixer until fluffy.

Dip 12 cookies into the milk or juice and place onto a suitable cake tray. Spread 2 to 3 Tablespoons of coconut whipped cream onto the cookie layer. Cut bananas into rather thin coins. Add one layer of banana coins onto the whipped cream layer. Now dip another 12 cookies and continue the same procedure until you have four layers of cookies. The last layer should be whipped cream and berries (you can also add berries to the middle layers). I also put whipped cream on the each side of the cake. Keep the cake in a cool place for at least a couple of hours or overnight before serving.

CHERRY AND ALMOND CHOCOLATE TRUFFLES

I really wanted to create a classic chocolate truffle recipe for this book. I also like raw and mixed dry fruit truffles, but my heart belongs to these succulent and slightly bitter dark chocolate cherry and almond truffles. To make it really simple, you can leave out the cherries and almonds, but they are definitely a match made in heaven!

Makes 25 medium truffles

- 10½ ounces vegan dark chocolate
- ¾ cup coconut milk
- 1 cup almonds
- 25 cherries, canned
- cocoa powder for coating

Break up the chocolate and put it into a bowl. Bring the coconut milk to boil and immediately pour it over the chocolate. Stir until the chocolate is dissolved. Add crushed almonds and stir again. Cover the bowl with plastic wrap and leave it to set in the fridge for at least 4 hours or overnight. Remove the bowl from the fridge.

Take one Tablespoon of the medium-soft chocolate mixture and place it in the palm of your hand. Make a tiny "pancake" out of this mixture. Place a cherry in the middle of the "pancake" and wrap the edges around the cherry. Roll the truffle in your hands until it is smooth and rounded. Now roll it in the cocoa powder. Continue until you are out of the chocolate mixture (a.k.a. *ganache*). I washed and dried my hands from time to time and then continued making truffles. You can store the truffles in the fridge or at room temperature.

HEDGEHOG SLICE

This super easy no-bake dessert has many cute names: cold dog cake, **kalter hund**, **Schwarzer Peter**, and **kalte schnauze**. In Estonia, kids love it and are taught the recipe at a very young age. This is my simple version. You can definitely add different dried and chopped fruits, nuts, crushed candy, and so on. I also added a little bit of strong liquor, but you can leave it out if you are serving it to the little ones.

Serves 8–10

- 17½ ounces vegan digestive cookies
- 9 ounces vegan margarine
- 3 Tablespoons brown sugar
- 2 Tablespoons cocoa powder
- 1¼ cups dark chocolate chips
- ½ Tablespoon strong liquor

Crush the cookies while leaving some lumps (I used a plastic bag and a rolling pin). Melt the margarine with sugar and add to the crushed cookies, along with cocoa powder, chocolate chips, and strong liquor. Mix well with your hands and form a chubby sausage out of the mixture. Roll the sausage tightly into the foil and leave it in the freezer for a couple of hours. Remove it from the freezer and let it melt for about 20 minutes at room temperature before slicing and serving.

CAKES, BARS, AND BREADS

BLUEBERRY JELLY CAKE

This is a very universal recipe and works every time I want to make a creamy and tasty jelly cake. I have tried it with different berries and fruits and it always comes out lovely. You can skip the vanilla cream but it will be juicier with it.

Makes one 10-inch cake

Crust:
- 2 cups all-purpose flour
- 4 Tablespoons sugar
- 5½ ounces vegan margarine, cut into cubes
- ¾ cup vegan vanilla custard (almost any thick custard will do)
- ½ cup coconut flakes

Jelly:
- 2 cups sweet liquid (This should be juice or berry syrup mixed with water. I used homemade cherry syrup and added water to it.)
- 2 teaspoons agar-agar powder
- berries or fruits of your choice

Preheat the oven to 400°F. Prepare the crust: mix the flour with sugar, add margarine cubes, and use your fingers to mix the margarine and flour until the dough becomes crumbly. If you pinch some of the crumbly dough and it holds together, it's ready. Put a round-sized piece of parchment paper in a 10-inch cake pan. (I put the cake pan on the parchment paper, drew out the exact size of the pan, and then cut it out.) Pour the crust dough into the cake pan and press onto the bottom with your fingers. Mix the vanilla cream with coconut flakes and pour it evenly on the crust (I used a spatula). Bake the crust for 20 minutes, cool it down, and add blueberries (or other berries and fruits) to it.

When the crust is cooled down, prepare the jelly: in a small pot, mix the agar-agar powder with sweet liquid. Then put the pot onto the stove and let the mixture boil for a few minutes. It has to boil hard so you can see the foam on top of it. Test it with a spoon—the mixture should also be pretty thick, almost like a syrup. Pour the mixture onto the cake and berries. Put the cake in a cold place and let the jelly get thick before serving.

SIMPLE CRUMB CAKE WITH APPLE JAM

Tasty, cheap, and easy—I love these three words in my cooking! And this cake is all of those. I really cannot think of an easier crumb cake recipe. You can use almost any kind of jam in this cake and it will be delicious. I recommend making this cake in a deep, medium-sized baking dish so it will be fluffy and soft rather than thin and crispy.

Makes one 12 x 9–inch crumb cake

- 3 cups whole-wheat flour
- ½ cup brown sugar
- 9 ounces vegan margarine
- 2 cups thick apple jam (or other jam of your preference)
- ½ teaspoon ground cinnamon

Preheat the oven to 400°F. Mix the dry ingredients (except cinnamon) and add chunks of margarine. Mix the flour with your fingers until you have a breadcrumb consistency. Cover the baking dish with parchment paper and pour in half of the dough crumbs. Push the crumbs gently onto the bottom. Now add apple jam and spread it evenly onto the crumbs. Spoon in the rest of the crumbs and spread them evenly onto the apple jam. Sprinkle some ground cinnamon on top. Bake for 30 to 35 minutes. Let it cool before cutting and serving.

CARROT AND PEANUT BUTTER BROWNIES

I rarely eat dessert (I'm more into fresh fruits), but who can say no to these chewy brownies? I also make my own peanut butter to go in the recipe, which is actually really simple! Just buy some salted and roasted peanuts and blend them with a food processor or hand blender until you have a smooth peanut butter—so much cheaper and with no extra unnecessary stuff.

Grated carrots make the brownies juicy, but other than that, you can barely tell they're there. And it is always better to bake the brownies for a somewhat smaller amount of time to keep from overcooking them. They are also perfect if you make them the night before and store them in the fridge, but to be honest, I couldn't wait that long!

Makes about 12 brownie squares

Batter:

- ¾ cup whole-wheat flour
- 4 Tablespoons all-purpose flour
- 2 teaspoons baking powder
- 4 Tablespoons cocoa powder
- ⅝ cup brown sugar
- 10 ounces carrots, grated
- 3½ ounces dark vegan chocolate, melted
- ⅖ cup water
- ¼ cup sunflower oil
- 1 teaspoon apple cider vinegar
- 3 Tablespoons peanut butter

Preheat the oven to 350°F. Mix the dry ingredients, and then add grated carrots, melted chocolate, water, oil, vinegar, and peanut butter. Mix until you have a smooth batter. Grease a deep 12 x 9 baking dish, cover the bottom with parchment paper, pour in the batter, and spread it evenly onto the bottom of the baking dish. Bake for 25 minutes. In the meantime, prepare the glaze.

Glaze:

- 3½ ounces dark vegan chocolate
- 2 Tablespoons peanut butter

Melt the chocolate, add peanut butter, and stir.

When the cake is baked, cover with glaze and let cool in the fridge for about 15 minutes or overnight before serving.

DECADENT PULL-APART CINNAMON BREAD

Who doesn't love cinnamon bread? And pull-apart cinnamon bread? And **decadent** pull-apart cinnamon bread? When I photographed this sweet bread and the last photo was taken, I just couldn't wait to take a huge bite. It contains a lot of marzipan, vanilla cream, dark chocolate, and hazelnuts. Perfect for a lovely family night or for special guests.

Makes 2 loaves

For the sweet yeast dough:
- 3 ⅔ cups all-purpose flour
- ½ teaspoon salt
- 4 Tablespoons dark muscovado sugar or regular brown sugar
- 2 Tablespoons active dry yeast
- 1 cup + 1 Tablespoon lukewarm soy milk
- 2½ ounces vegan margarine (room temperature) or 3 Tablespoons oil

Mix the dry ingredients. Add soy milk, stir, and then add soft margarine. Mix with your hands and knead hard on a floured surface until the dough is elastic. Put the dough ball in a bowl and cover the bowl with a clean kitchen towel. Leave in a warm place to rise for about 45 minutes.

For the marzipan and vanilla cream:
- 7 ounces vegan marzipan mass
- 1½ cups vegan vanilla custard
- ½ teaspoon vanilla extract

Take a non-stick pan and add grated marzipan, vanilla custard, and vanilla extract. Stir and simmer at low to medium heat for a couple of minutes. Remove from heat and set aside.

For the cinnamon glaze:
- 2¾ ounces vegan margarine
- 4 Tablespoons dark muscovado sugar or regular brown sugar
- ½ Tablespoon cinnamon powder

Melt the margarine and mix in the sugar and cinnamon powder.

For serving:
- 7 ounces peeled hazelnuts
- 3½ ounces dark vegan chocolate

Preheat the oven to 350°F. After the dough has risen, knead it on a floured surface and roll it until you have a wide rectangle. Spread the cinnamon glaze evenly on the rolled-out dough. Then spread the vanilla and marzipan cream on the cinnamon glaze. Slice the dough vertically into long strips (about 2 inches wide). Now stack the strips on top of each other (you will probably get a little messy since there is a lot of cream involved). Slice them into stacks of dough squares (about 2 inches wide). Now stack the dough squares into two greased 10 x 5 loaf pans like a flip-book. Let the dough rise under a kitchen towel in a warm place for 30 to 45 minutes. Preheat the oven to 350°F. Bake the loaves in the oven for 30 to 35 minutes until darker golden brown. Remove the cinnamon breads from the oven, and drizzle with melted dark chocolate and chopped hazelnuts. Let them cool for 20 minutes before cutting and serving.

MY MOM'S BLUEBERRY MUFFINS

My mom is an amazing baker. I have learned so much from her, so I just had to include her blueberry muffin recipe in this book. These muffins are simple yet incredibly tasty. If you can't use blueberries, you can replace them with berries of your choice. Even the next day, these muffins are really tasty and fluffy. Sprinkle with some powdered sugar to give them a more festive look.

Makes 12 muffins

- ¾ cup sugar
- 5 ⅓ ounces vegan margarine
- 1 ripe banana
- ⅖ cup hot water
- 1 ⅓ cups all-purpose flour
- 2 teaspoons baking powder
- ¾ cup oat flour
- 1 teaspoon flax meal
- ¾ cup blueberries
- powdered sugar (optional)

Preheat the oven to 400°F. Whip the sugar with margarine (I used a hand mixer). Add sliced banana and whip until smooth. Add hot water and stir. Add all-purpose flour mixed with baking powder. Add oat flour mixed with flax meal. Stir gently. Add about one Tablespoon of batter to each muffin cup. Place one teaspoon of blueberries into the center of each muffin cup. Now place one Tablespoon of batter onto the blueberries in each muffin cup. Bake for 20 to 25 minutes. Let muffins cool and sprinkle with powdered sugar if desired.

CURD PASTRY
WITH RAISINS

This delicious recipe is a traditional pastry from the region of Estonia in which I grew up. It is originally made with curd from cow's milk, but I replaced it with homemade tofu curd. If you don't have time to make your own tofu curd, you can use regular store-bought tofu.

Makes 18 little pies

For the sweet yeast dough:
- 3 ⅓ cups all-purpose flour
- ½ teaspoon salt
- 2 Tablespoons sugar
- 2 Tablespoons active dry yeast
- 1 cup + 1 Tablespoon lukewarm soy milk
- 2½ ounces vegan margarine (room temperature) or 3 Tablespoons oil

Mix the dry ingredients. Add soy milk, stir, and then add soft margarine. Mix with your hands and knead hard on a floured surface until the dough is elastic. Put the dough ball into a bowl and cover the bowl with a clean kitchen towel. Leave in a warm place to rise for about 45 minutes. In the meantime, prepare the tofu curd.

For the homemade tofu curd:
- 8 cups + 4 Tablespoons soy milk
- 1 teaspoon citric acid
- 1½ teaspoons vanilla sugar
- 3 Tablespoons sugar
- 4 Tablespoons melted vegan margarine
- 1 teaspoon grated lemon zest
- ¾ cups raisins

Bring 8 cups of the soy milk to boil (be careful, it can boil over really fast). Remove from heat. Add citric acid and gently stir it in. Let sit for about 5 to 10 minutes until the curds are separated. Skim out the curds and move them into a mesh bag or cloth. Squeeze hard until all the liquids are gone. Pour the drained curds into a bowl, and add vanilla sugar, regular sugar, melted margarine, grated lemon zest, and 4 Tablespoons of soy milk. Blend until smooth (I used a hand blender). Mix in the raisins. Now you have a tasty curd cream. You can also skip making the curd yourself and just use 2 cups crumbled tofu as a cream base.

Preheat your oven to 400°F. Place the risen yeast dough on a floured surface and knead for a couple of minutes. Cut it in half and form two long sausages. Cut the sausages into 18 equal coins. Make little dough balls out of the coins and put them onto a baking pan covered with parchment paper. Let the little balls rise for 30 more minutes. Now use a small circular object (a drinking glass for example), pressing it on each dough ball to form a hollow in the center. Add about 1 teaspoon of curd filling into the hollow area of each dough ball. Bake for 20 minutes. The curd pastries can be served with a fresh jam of your choice if desired.

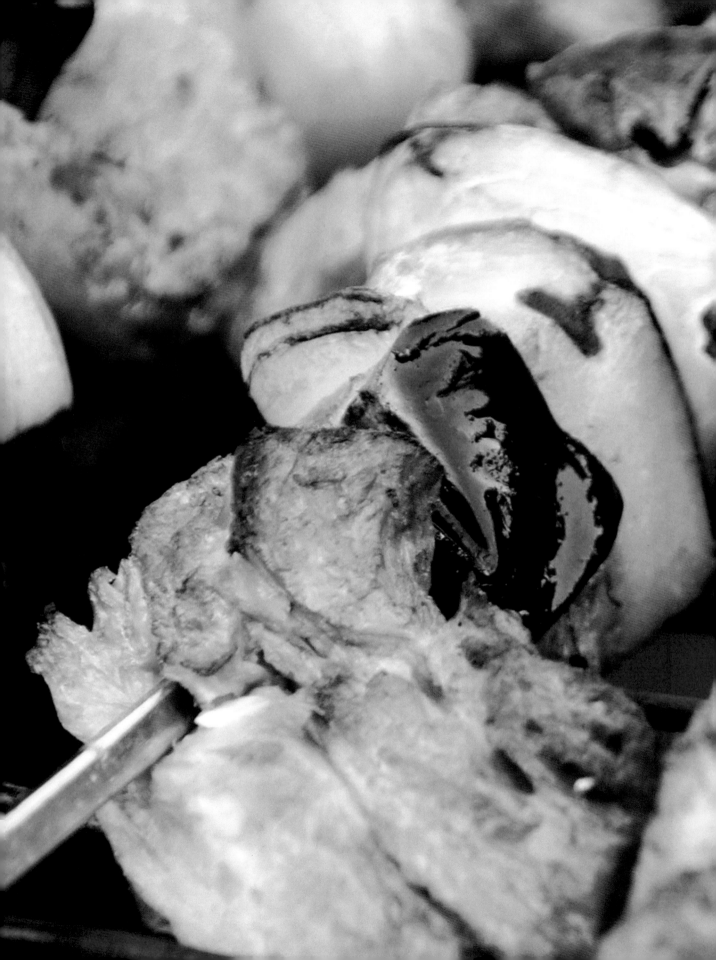

BARBECUE SPECIAL

CHICKPEA, BAKED BEET, AND PEANUT BUTTER PATTIES

I really wanted my barbecue burgers to be special, and you cannot go wrong with chickpeas and peanut butter. And these sweet little baked beet chunks were just divine. These patties are really nice on the grill. Just make sure the grill tray is really hot and properly greased before putting the patties on it.

Serves 8–10

- 2 cups dry chickpeas
- 3 cups uncooked beet cubes
- 2 Tablespoons oil
- ½ teaspoon salt
- pinch of ground black pepper
- 4 teaspoons peanut butter (For homemade peanut butter, blend salted and roasted peanuts until smooth.)
- 1 cup hot water
- ¾ teaspoon salt
- 6 Tablespoons your favorite smoky vegan barbecue sauce
- ¾ cup breadcrumbs

Soak the chickpeas for 10 to 12 hours. Boil until completely soft. In the meantime, preheat you oven to 400°F. Mix the beet cubes with oil, salt, and pepper. Cover with foil and bake for 20 minutes. Then remove the foil and bake for another 20 minutes. Drain and rinse the cooked chickpeas. In a large bowl, mix drained chickpeas with peanut butter, hot water, salt, and barbecue sauce. Blend with a hand blender until smooth. Add breadcrumbs and baked beet cubes. Mix with your hands. Form patties and grill on both sides.

VEGGIE AND SOY SKEWERS

These skewers are so satisfying and really fun to make. You can use different fresh herbs and add your favorite spices to this marinade. The outcome will always be delicious. I love to use these grilled soy chunks and veggies as a topping on the Grilled Pizza (see page 110).

Serves 4

- 4½ ounces dried soy cutlets
- 1 onion
- 1 eggplant
- 1 zucchini
- 4 cloves of garlic
- 4 Tablespoons oil
- 2 Tablespoons apple cider vinegar
- 1½ Tablespoons brown sugar
- ⅖ cup water
- 1 teaspoon turmeric
- 1 teaspoon ground cumin
- 2 teaspoons curry powder
- ½ teaspoon dried thyme
- 1–2 teaspoons vegetable stock powder
- 1-2 Tablespoons soy sauce

Boil the dried soy cutlets until soft, rinse with cold water, and squeeze out the extra water. Chop the onions and cut the eggplant and zucchini into cubes. Mix crushed garlic, oil, vinegar, sugar, and water with all the spices, vegetable stock powder, and soy sauce for the marinade. Mix the soy cutlets, chopped onions, eggplant cubes, and zucchini cubes with marinade and leave them in the fridge to marinate for a couple of hours or overnight. Thread the cutlets and veggies onto the skewers and grill until crispy.

GRILLED PIZZA

For years, I had no idea that grilling a pizza could be so easy! It's really simple and adds so much to your vegan barbecue. I used Veggie and Soy Skewers as a topping (see page 108), but you can use any of your favorite or seasonal veggies.

Makes 2 large pizzas, 4 medium pizzas, or 8 small pizzas

For the crust:
- 2 cups all-purpose flour
- 1 cup whole-wheat flour
- ½ teaspoon salt
- ½ teaspoon dried thyme
- 2 Tablespoons oil
- 1 cup hot water

In a large bowl, mix flours with salt and thyme. Add oil and mix it with flour using your fingers. Add half of the water, mix, add the remaining half, and mix with your hands until you get a dough ball. When the dough ball doesn't stick to your fingers anymore, put it in the plastic wrap and let sit for 10 minutes. In the meantime, prepare the toppings.

For the toppings:
- veggie and soy skewers or any of your favorite grilled veggies
- 1–2 Tablespoons oil for each pizza crust
- 2–3 Tablespoons ketchup or tomato sauce for each pizza crust

You can make 8 small, 4 medium, or 2 large pizzas out of this dough. I like to make a few medium ones. Just divide the dough ball into equal balls, roll the balls wide, and then sprinkle oil onto each crust. Cover the grill tray with an oiled foil and put the crusts on it. Grill on both sides until crispy. Add ketchup or tomato sauce to each crust and then add the toppings. Serve immediately.

BAKED BEANS

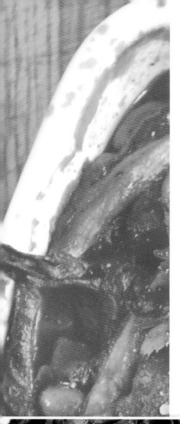

I wanted to make my baked beans a little bit special. My first plan was to add eggplant to this recipe. But for some reason, the stores were all out of eggplants that day. So I decided to add yellow wax beans and green beans instead. I must say that the outcome was truly amazing. My whole family raved after eating two portions—and still wanted more! Baking the beans in the oven definitely makes a difference and adds so much to the texture and flavor. This dish is great both on summer barbecue nights and on a crispy winter night.

Serves 6–8

- 4 Tablespoons oil
- 3 onions
- 2½ teaspoons salt
- ground black pepper to taste
- ½ teaspoon ground nutmeg
- 3 teaspoons paprika powder
- 2 Tablespoons brown sugar
- 14 ounces green beans (I used frozen)
- 16 ounces yellow beans
- ½ cup water
- 14 ounces canned white beans
- 14 ounces canned kidney beans
- 2 cups tomato paste
- 1½ cups tomato juice

Preheat the oven to 400°F. Heat oil in a wok or in a thick-bottomed pot. Add sliced onions, salt, pepper, and nutmeg. Cook until the onions are golden brown. Add paprika powder and brown sugar. Cook for a couple of minutes until the sugar is caramelized. Add green and yellow beans. Cook for a couple of minutes and add water. Simmer for 10 minutes. Add drained and rinsed white beans and kidney beans along with tomato paste and tomato juice. Stir and simmer for 10 to 15 minutes. Pour the beans into a deep greased baking pan. Bake for 45 minutes. Garnish with fresh herbs.

CREAMY CORN AND SAUERKRAUT SALAD

This creamy corn and sauerkraut salad was a big hit at one of my vegan barbecues. It went so well with crispy veggie sausages. I balanced the sauerkraut's acidity with some brown sugar.

Serves 4–6

- 10½ ounces canned corn
- 12 ounces uncooked sauerkraut
- 5 Tablespoons vegan mayo or ranch dressing
- salt and pepper to taste
- 3 teaspoons brown sugar

Drain the corn and mix well with other ingredients.

RICH SALAD WITH TOFU SCRAMBLE

This salad is more like a snack platter. It has so many delicious ingredients. Hearty tofu scramble, grilled veggies, juicy lettuce, olives, and tangy sun-dried tomatoes. I made this rich salad for my mom's birthday barbecue and she really loved it.

Serves 4–6

- 2–3 Tablespoons oil
- 9 ounces firm tofu
- 2–3 teaspoons curry powder
- 1 Tablespoon soy sauce
- 2 red onions (sliced and mixed with some soy sauce and balsamic vinegar)
- 1 medium-sized can of artichoke hearts
- some chopped lettuce
- a couple of handfuls of arugula
- ½ cup sun-dried tomatoes in oil
- ½ cup black pitted olives
- 2 Tablespoons vegan ranch dressing or mayo
- 2 Tablespoons of oil

Heat oil in a pan, and add crumbled tofu, curry powder, and soy sauce. Cook for a couple of minutes and then remove from heat. Grill the onion slices and drained artichoke hearts. Place all the ingredients on a platter and drizzle some vegan mayo or ranch on top.

GRILLED PEACH HALVES WITH WHIPPED CREAM AND CHOCOLATE

Grilling is not only limited to savory food, and, oh my, these grilled peaches are amazing. I drool every time I look at the pictures. Perfectly delightful and a really sweet ending to this marvelous vegan barbecue feast.

Serves 4–6

- 2 (29-ounce) cans peaches
- store-bought vegan whipped cream or your own homemade coconut whipped cream (see recipe for Estonian Cookie Cake on page 84)
- 3½ ounces dark vegan chocolate
- crushed nuts for serving (optional)

Drain the peaches, reserving about half a can of the liquid. Grill the peach halves on both sides. Melt the chocolate and mix in the reserved peach liquid. Put about 2 to 3 peach halves on a plate, add some coconut whipped cream, and drizzle with melted chocolate and crushed nuts if desired. It is best to use a fork while eating them!

CHRISTMAS SPECIAL

BLACK PUDDING SAUSAGES

In Estonia, there is a tradition of eating black pudding sausages every year for Christmas. And since I like the main dishes to really stand out, especially on Christmas, I just had to create a vegan version of these sausages, which are usually made of blood, barley, and guts (yikes!). My sausages are so much better! The only problem was figuring out what to use to replace the guts, which hold the sausage together. My boyfriend came up with an idea to use nori sheets instead. I was a bit skeptical, since I was afraid the taste of nori would be too dominant, but that wasn't the case at all. They fit perfectly and now I can share this tasty recipe with you.

Makes about 10 sausages

- 3 Tablespoons oil
- 1 large onion
- ½ teaspoon salt
- 2 teaspoons dried marjoram
- ¾ teaspoon ground nutmeg
- 2 teaspoons dried rosemary
- ¼ teaspoon ground cinnamon
- 4 Tablespoons soy sauce
- 4 cups barley porridge (unseasoned, thick and made of cracked barley groats)
- 14 ounces canned black beans (any other bean will be fine too)
- 4 Tablespoons whole-wheat or barley flour
- 1½ teaspoons vegetable stock powder
- 10 nori leaves

Preheat the oven to 400°F. Heat oil in a pan and add finely chopped onions and salt. Cook for a couple of minutes. Add dried marjoram, ground nutmeg, dried rosemary, and cinnamon. Mix and cook for a minute. Add soy sauce and cook for another minute. Remove from heat and add the fried onion mix to the barley porridge. Drain and rinse the black beans, mash with a fork, and add to the barley porridge as well. Add flour and vegetable stock powder. Now, spread about 2 to 3 tablespoons of barley filling evenly onto each nori sheet. Turn the left and right sides of the sheets inside and roll the sheet into a sausage until you reach the end of the sheet. Continue this procedure with every nori sheet until you are out of the filling. Put the sausages on a greased baking tray and brush each sausage with a little bit of oil. Bake for 20 to 25 minutes. They are also very tasty the next day when warmed up. They can be served with lingonberry jam if desired.

LENTIL AND PUMPKIN LOAF

A proper lentil loaf recipe is a must-have in the vegan kitchen. I wanted to make this loaf gluten free, delicious, and firm rather than mushy on the inside. It is great served with hearty dishes, like crispy baked potatoes and creamy chili bean and zucchini stew. It is also delicious on a sandwich with a dash of mild mustard.

Makes 1 loaf

- 3 Tablespoons flax meal
- 9 Tablespoons water
- 1 cup uncooked green lentils
- ½ cup uncooked rice
- 2–3 Tablespoons oil
- 2 onions
- 1 teaspoon salt
- pinch of ground black pepper
- 3 cloves of garlic
- 1½ cups grated pumpkin
- 3 Tablespoons rice flour
- 2 teaspoons vegetable stock powder
- 4 Tablespoons nutritional yeast (optional)
- 2 Tablespoons corn starch
- 1 teaspoon baking powder
- ½ teaspoon dried rosemary
- 1 teaspoon apple cider vinegar
- 3 Tablespoons your favorite vegan barbecue sauce or quality ketchup for glazing

Preheat the oven to 350°F. Prepare the flax "eggs" by mixing the flax meal with water. Leave it in the refrigerator for at least 15 minutes.

Boil the lentils and rice together until soft and even a little overcooked. In the meantime, heat oil in a pan and add chopped onions, salt, and pepper. Cook for about 2–3 minutes until golden brown. Add chopped garlic, cook for 30 seconds, and then add grated pumpkin. Cook for a couple of minutes. Drain the lentils and rice very well, so all the liquids are gone. Mix boiled and drained lentils and rice with fried onions and pumpkin. Mix dry ingredients (rice flour, stock powder, nutritional yeast, corn starch, baking powder, and dried rosemary) in a large bowl. Add the mixed dry ingredients to the lentil mix along with apple cider vinegar. Mix very carefully.

Grease a 10 x 5 loaf pan and pour in the batter. Smooth it with a spoon, add barbecue sauce or ketchup, and spread it evenly onto the loaf. Bake for 45 to 50 minutes. Let cool before serving. This photo was taken after the loaf had been in the fridge overnight.

CABBAGE, BEET, AND APPLE STEW

In some video games, like in Skyrim, you can actually cook food. In Skyrim, in a cozy log cabin, you can prepare different hearty stews in a large kettle. This stew is as cozy and tasty as it would be in that video game, only better—you can actually eat it! The best time for this stew is definitely Christmas.

Serves 4–6

- 3 Tablespoons oil
- 1 onion
- 1½–2 teaspoons salt
- 3 cups uncooked beets cut into little cubes
- 2 bay leaves
- 1¾ cups water
- 3½ cups shredded cabbage
- 2 cups sliced apples

Heat oil in a thick-bottomed pot and add chopped onions and salt. Cook for about 2 minutes. Add beet cubes, bay leaves, and water. Boil over medium heat covered until the beets are half cooked. Add shredded cabbage and boil until the cabbage is soft. Add sliced apples and boil until the beets and apples are soft. Remove from heat and serve with side or main dishes of your choice.

SWEET POTATO AND MUSHROOM PIE

In Estonia, sweet potatoes aren't very common. They sell them only at large supermarkets, and most people would rather buy regular potatoes for their price and familiar taste. But when I thought of a pie suitable for Christmas, it just had to contain sweet potatoes. I personally love these bright orange fellas, and this creamy, flavorful, and filling pie will definitely compliment your holiday dinner.

Makes one 11-inch pie

- 17 ⅓ ounces vegan puff pastry
- 1¾ pounds uncooked sweet potatoes
- 2 Tablespoons oil
- 5 cups chopped white mushrooms
- salt and pepper to taste
- ¼ teaspoon dried thyme
- ½ Tablespoon lemon juice
- 4 Tablespoons vegan cream

Place the frozen dough in the refrigerator the night before you intend to bake it. Wash but don't peel the sweet potatoes, and boil them until soft. Preheat the oven to 400°F. Heat oil in a pan and add chopped white mushrooms, salt, pepper, and dried thyme. Cook for about 5 minutes, or until the mushrooms have released their juices. When the potatoes are soft, drain them and rinse with cold water. Peel the potatoes and chop into smaller cubes. Add the potato cubes to the mushrooms along with lemon juice and vegan cream. Stir and cook for a couple of minutes. Taste for salt, and then remove from heat. Grease an 11-inch round cake pan. Roll out the puff pastry on a floured surface and cut into two equal squares. Place one square onto the bottom of the cake pan and pinch the edges until smoother and more rounded. Add the filling and then place the second puff pastry square onto the top of the filling. Crimp the bottom and upper pastry edges together and smooth a little bit with your fingers. Bake for 45 minutes. Let cool slightly before cutting and serving.

CHUNKY MUSHROOM AND PLUM GRAVY

At first, I wanted to make this gravy smooth. But when I saw how beautifully chunky it was, I just couldn't bring myself to blend it. Of course, you can always do that to make it smoother or to get your kid to eat some mushrooms. This gravy is perfect with mashed potatoes or potatoes of any kind. The dried plums really give a rich and kind of smoky flavor and texture.

Serves 4–6

- 3 Tablespoons oil
- 2 onions
- 1½–2 teaspoons salt
- pinch of ground black pepper
- 1 cup dried plums
- 5 cups chopped white mushrooms
- ½ cup water
- ¾ cup vegan cream
- fresh herbs for garnish (optional)

Heat oil in a thick-bottomed pot. Add chopped onions, salt, and pepper. Cook for a couple of minutes until onions are golden brown. Add chopped dried plums and cook for a minute. Add chopped mushrooms and water. Simmer over medium heat covered for about 5 to 7 minutes. Add cream and simmer for another 2 minutes. Garnish with fresh herbs, if you like.

SAUERKRAUT WITH BARLEY

Sauerkraut with barley is a very common dish in Estonia, especially in the south where I grew up. Adding barley to the sauerkraut makes the dish really filling and tasty, and it is even suitable to serve as a main dish with baked potatoes on the side.

Serves 4–6

- 2–3 Tablespoons oil
- 2 onions
- 4½ cups uncooked sauerkraut (mine had some grated carrots in it, too)
- ¾ cup uncooked barley groats
- 8 cups water
- 1½ teaspoons salt
- pinch of ground black pepper
- 3 Tablespoons brown sugar

Heat oil in a thick-bottomed pot. Add chopped onions and cook for a couple of minutes. Add sauerkraut, rinsed barley, and water. Stir and boil over medium heat covered for about 1½ hours. Add salt, pepper, and brown sugar. Stir and boil for 5 more minutes. Remove from heat and let cool slightly before serving.

MILD MUSTARD SAUCE

This rich and creamy sauce is a super quick and perfect addition to a holiday table. Serve it with other hearty Christmas dishes, like mashed potatoes or Lentil and Pumpkin Loaf (see page 124).

Serves 4–6

- 1 cup vegan cream
- 1½ Tablespoons mild mustard
- chopped fresh dill
- 1 Tablespoon soy sauce

In a sauce pan, mix all the ingredients, bring to a boil, and then remove from heat.

WARMING SPICED PUNCH

This tangy sip is seriously warming. Serve it to the freezing guests who have come through a snow storm, and you will immediately see the color coming back to their faces. This punch is best when using only quality juices with no added sugars.

Serves 4–6

- 1 thumb-sized piece of ginger root
- 3 Tablespoons brown sugar
- 1½ cups hot water
- 4¼ cups pomegranate juice
- 2 cups pineapple juice
- grated lemon zest (optional)

Peel the ginger root and cut it into tiny pieces. Put the chopped ginger root, brown sugar, and water into a pot. Bring to a boil and let simmer for 10 minutes. Add pomegranate juice, pineapple juice, and some grated lemon zest if you want, and let it simmer for another 15 minutes. Serve in a mug or in a hot drink glass.

SOFT GINGERBREAD CAKE WITH CHOCOLATE AND PEANUT BUTTER GLAZE

*I just **love** soft gingerbread. And a whole soft gingerbread cake is even more amazing, especially with chocolate and peanut butter glaze. My mom and I eat this cake like there's no tomorrow. And you can add dried fruits and nuts to make it even richer. A perfect Christmas cake!*

1 10-inch cake

For the cake:
- 2½ cups all-purpose flour
- 1 teaspoon baking powder
- 1 teaspoon baking soda
- 5 Tablespoons brown sugar
- 2 teaspoons gingerbread spice mix
- 1½ cups water
- 1 teaspoon (apple cider) vinegar
- 3 Tablespoons peanut butter
- ¼ cups oil (I used sunflower oil)

Glaze:
- 7 ounces dark vegan chocolate
- 2–3 Tablespoons peanut butter

Preheat the oven to 350°F. Mix the dry ingredients. Add water, vinegar, peanut butter, and oil. Mix carefully and pour the batter into a 10-inch greased cake pan. Bake for 40 minutes.

Prepare the glaze: melt the chocolate in a water bath, add peanut butter, and stir. When the cake is baked, take it out of the oven and remove the baking pan. Glaze the cake and let cool before serving.

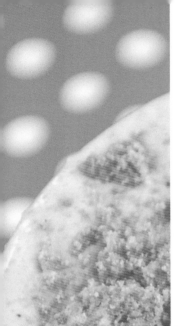

GINGERBREAD ICE CREAM SHAKE

This ice-cream shake is to die for—it is so divine! I created this recipe many years ago and it is still one of my favorites. If you are feeling a little naughty, you can use regular mulled wine instead of non-alcoholic.

Serves 3–4

- 14 ounces vegan vanilla ice-cream
- 2 cups chilled non-alcoholic mulled wine
- 6–7 gingerbread cookies + more for serving

Blend all the ingredients until smooth. Serve right away with some crushed gingerbread cookies.

CONVERSION CHARTS

Metric and Imperial Conversions
(These conversions are rounded for convenience)

Ingredient	Cups/Tablespoons/Teaspoons	Ounces	Grams/Milliliters
Butter	1 cup/ 16 tablespoons/ 2 sticks	8 ounces	230 grams
Cheese, shredded	1 cup	4 ounces	110 grams
Cornstarch	1 tablespoon	0.3 ounce	8 grams
Cream cheese	1 tablespoon	0.5 ounce	14.5 grams
Flour, all-purpose	1 cup/1 tablespoon	4.5 ounces/0.3 ounce	125 grams/8 grams
Flour, whole wheat	1 cup	4 ounces	120 grams
Fruit, dried	1 cup	4 ounces	120 grams
Fruits or veggies, chopped	1 cup	5 to 7 ounces	145 to 200 grams
Fruits or veggies, pureed	1 cup	8.5 ounces	245 grams
Honey, maple syrup, or corn syrup	1 tablespoon	0.75 ounce	20 grams
Liquids: cream, milk, water, or juice	1 cup	8 fluid ounces	240 milliliters
Oats	1 cup	5.5 ounces	150 grams
Salt	1 teaspoon	0.2 ounce	6 grams
Spices: cinnamon, cloves, ginger, or nutmeg (ground)	1 teaspoon	0.2 ounce	5 milliliters
Sugar, brown, firmly packed	1 cup	7 ounces	200 grams
Sugar, white	1 cup/1 tablespoon	7 ounces/0.5 ounce	200 grams/12.5 grams
Vanilla extract	1 teaspoon	0.2 ounce	4 grams

Oven Temperatures

Fahrenheit	Celsius	Gas Mark
225°	110°	¼
250°	120°	½
275°	140°	1
300°	150°	2
325°	160°	3
350°	180°	4
375°	190°	5
400°	200°	6
425°	220°	7
450°	230°	8

INDEX